knitted together

Eight Bible Study Sessions
and
Knitting Patterns for Baby Gifts

knitted together

Julie Stiegemeyer and Sara Nordling

A Women's Small-Group Bible Study

CONCORDIA PUBLISHING HOUSE · SAINT LOUIS

Copyright © 2011 Concordia Publishing House
3558 S. Jefferson Avenue, St. Louis, MO 63118-3968
1-800-325-3040 • www.cph.org

All rights reserved. Unless specifically noted, no part of this publication may be reproduced, stored in a retrieval system, or transmitted, in any form or by any means, electronic, mechanical, photocopying, recording, or otherwise, without the prior written permission of Concordia Publishing House.

Written by Julie Stiegemeyer
Patterns by Sara Nordling

Scripture quotations from the ESV Bible® (The Holy Bible, English Standard Version®), copyright © 2001 by Crossway Bibles, a publishing ministry of Good News Publishers. Used by permission. All rights reserved.

The quotation marked AE 12 in this publication is from Luther's Works, the American Edition: vol. 12 © 1955 by Concordia Publishing House, all rights reserved.

The quotation marked AE 35 in this publication is from Luther's Works, the American Edition: vol. 35 © 1960 by Muhlenberg Press. Used by permission of Augsburg Fortress.

Manufactured in the United States of America.

2 3 4 5 6 7 8 9 10 11   21 20 19 18 17 16 15 14 13 12

*This study is dedicated with thanksgiving
to my women's Bible study group
at Redeemer Lutheran Church in Elmhurst, Illinois.
I thank God for your support and
love as sisters in Christ.*

*It is also dedicated to all those
who carry on the knitting tradition.*

—J.S. and S.N.

Table of Contents

General Directions for Knitters   8

Suggestions for Small-Group Participants   9

Introduction   11

Session 1: Those Tiny Toenails!   15
    Baby Booties   21

Session 2: Wrapped in God's Love   23
    Easy Blanket   28

Session 3: Soggy Babies   29
    Shell-Stitch Blanket   35

Session 4: Life to the Fullest   37
    Sheep Toy   42

Session 5: Shelter from the Storm   46
    Easy Hat   53

Session 6: The Ordinary and the Extraordinary   55
    Baptism Shell Washcloth   61

Session 7: What Your Hand Finds to Do   65
    Bath Mitt   71

Session 8: Numbering the Hairs on Our Heads   73
    Difficult Hat   78

Conclusion   81

Leader's Notes   85

General Directions for Knitters

This book is, first and foremost, a small-group Bible study developed to direct you to the Scriptures and to give witness to the Gospel in all aspects of life. It's also a little collection of patterns for baby projects. Combining a Bible study with knitting patterns seems like a likely thing to do because both knitters and those who participate in Bible study rarely do so in isolation. We are created for community, after all. And our participation in and appreciation for both activities are deepened when we join with others who share these passions.

The developers of this book assume that you already have some knowledge of knitting techniques, so we have not included step-by-step directions for how to do that. But we offer here some information to help you get started with these projects.

Tools used

Needles: Straight, circular, and double-pointed in varying sizes, and a yarn or tapestry needle for weaving in ends

Crochet hook
Tape measure
Scissors
Stitch markers

Suggested yarns

We suggest that you consider how these items will be used before you begin shopping for yarn. You'll want to use yarns that will be soft and comforting against baby's skin. Equally important, baby items should be made from durable yarn that holds up to laundering. Acrylics and cottons work well. Wools, silks, and novelty yarns do not. Two of the items (baby bath mitt and washcloth) must be made from cotton yarn. Yarn weight depends on the pattern and size of needles, of course, but all of these items are made with fingering- and sport-weight yarns. These patterns are for useful, even utilitarian, baby items and not heirloom or keepsake gifts. Brands and weights are suggested for each pattern.

Stitch terms used

Cast on
Bind off
K = Knit
P = Purl
YO = Yarn over (to increase)
M1 = Make one (to increase)
K2tog = Knit two stitches together (to decrease)
P2tog = Purl two stitches together (to decrease)
S1 = Slip one stitch
SSK = Slip, slip, knit
PSSO = Pass slipped stitch over
DPN = Double pointed needle(s)
Garter stitch = knit all stitches
Stockinette stitch = knit on the front side of the item, and purl on the back side
* = indicates the beginning of a series of stitches to repeat
Turn = Literally, to turn your knitting around so you begin knitting the next row

About gauge

All of these patterns provide a gauge to ensure that your finished piece is similar in size and shape to the designer's original. The gauge is not as important for items such as the blankets or washcloth, but it is very important when making the other items. Always be on the safe side and knit a gauge swatch.

When you need help

If you get stuck, we recommend that you consult with your sister knitters, turn to a good knitting book, or search online for knitting tips. While we don't endorse a specific book or site, there are many helpful resources available to you.

Suggestions for Small-Group Participants

1. Begin small-group time with prayer.
2. Everyone should feel free to express her thoughts. Comments shared in the small group should remain confidential unless you have received permission to share them outside your group.
3. If your meeting time does not allow you to discuss all of the questions for the week, the leader should choose the questions most meaningful to the group.
4. Close by sharing concerns and prayer requests, then praying together.

"O Lord, You have searched me and known me!"

In these very few words at the opening of Psalm 139, we discover some extraordinary things about God. Look at the verse again. What does it tell you? What is God saying to you today in these few words?

One thing we learn about is God's knowledge. What does He know? These words show us that God is omnipotent: He knows all. This verse describes God's knowledge of every person. He has "searched" and "known" us.

What else? Look at the verse again.

Whom does God know? He knows us. God is personal. He shows His interest in individuals and, even further, He is interested in each one of us. This is unusual when you consider people in the past and their experience with other (false) gods. Think of the priests of Baal who on Mount Carmel slashed their skin and bled to try to get the attention of their false god. Think of the endless wheels of prayer that Buddhists spin hour upon hour to try to elicit the answer to their petition. But in these very few words from Psalm 139, we find something very different. We find that we have a Father in heaven who is infinitely interested in each one of us, who cares enough to search and know us, who sees us as worthy to be knowable.

One other thing from these few words stands out. Does this verse show people reaching up to God, seeking His attention, searching Him out? No. It shows us that God takes the initiative; He reaches down to us, searches us and knows us.

We can learn so much from just a few words in Scripture, can't we? Some things we maybe never thought about before; other things we've known but have taken for granted.

About a year ago, I went to a short workshop on interpersonal communication. The college professor who was leading the talk gave the group a task. We had to pair up and listen—really listen—to our partner talk about an event in the past that had made a big impact on him or her. We had to listen so carefully, in fact, that then we would repeat the highlights of the other's experience to the group. While we were listening, we could only ask clarifying questions and not interject any of our own thoughts or experiences.

It was a fascinating exercise because it taught me to "zip the lip," if only for a few minutes. Whenever I talk to people, I love to share something similar in my own life. But is that really listening? Maybe it's just an example of me liking the sound of my own voice or enjoying my own experiences again while not really listening to the other person. Through this activity, though, by consciously and carefully listening to each other, a strong connection was formed between a stranger and me. We shared an important moment, listened, and really connected.

Our human connections are always tainted by sin. We have to be taught how to listen and, at least on occasion, zip it. There's nothing wrong with sharing similar experiences; this is how we connect. But what usually happens is that we are too wrapped up in our own thoughts to concentrate on another individual.

But God is not that way. He searches us. He knows us, individually, personally. He wants to hear the sound of our voice, the concerns that weigh on us, the burdens and the joys of whatever may be in our hearts.

Psalm 139 goes on to show just how intimately God knows us: "For You formed my inward parts; You knitted me together in my mother's womb. I praise You, for I am fearfully and wonderfully made. Wonderful are Your works; my soul knows it very well" (vv. 13–14). God not only knows us, but He also made us, intricately, delicately, intimately.

I took up knitting a couple of years ago and was taught by Sara Nordling, who created the patterns for this study. I fumbled around with my needles and yarn for my first couple of projects and then, as time went on, I started to see some beautiful patterns emerge from my hands.

What I find fascinating about knitting is that there are no knots in the patterns. It's really just one piece of yarn, turned and twisted and looped and tucked into beautiful patterns. From this one strand of yarn, a garment is created, loop by loop and row by row. And at the end, when I finally ease the last loops off the needle, I know this project inside and out. I made it, humble though it may be. I see the mistakes, the details, the colors, and the pattern in a way no one else will ever see it.

This is, perhaps, a small glimpse into the way God knit us together. He formed us. He shaped us. And He continues to use experiences in our daily lives to recreate us into His disciples and reassure us of His grace and favor. He knows the details, the hopes, the fears, the loves, and the hurts better than anyone else ever could.

This Bible study is unique in that, along with the Bible readings and questions and answers, your group also can work together to create some beautiful projects to give away to a local crisis pregnancy center or use as Baptism gifts in your congregation or in some other way you might choose. We women are great multitaskers, so this should be no sweat. Through each project and each week of your study, learn and trust that God knows you as your Maker, your Redeemer, and your closest friend and advocate. God knows you intimately, as the One who made you and shaped you into the wonderful creation you are today. And even better than that, He has recreated you in the redeeming work of Christ.

So, knit away! And enjoy the promise that God, who knit you together, knows you, cares for you, and loves you as His perfect creation!

Julie Stiegemeyer

Those Tiny Toenails!

As a young mom, I marveled at the tiny fingers and toes of my baby. These perfectly formed hands and feet in miniature amazed me. The soft half-moon of a tiny toenail. The spreading, bending, grabbing fingers. The fingernails, soft but sharp enough to scratch his little face.

Recently, I was looking through my son's baby book and turned to the page with his footprint. Five toes, an arch, a heel, with ridges and wrinkles, in a little imprint on the page, representing all those precious memories of his babyhood. That little baby now is taller than me, and every day I see glimpses of the man he will soon become. But I will never forget that overwhelming sense of awe and wonder as I studied this little one's perfect toes and fingers in the days after he was born. It amazed me to think of God's perfect creation and my role as mother and caregiver to this tiny little one.

I remember one afternoon in particular when my son was maybe a month old. He was still small enough to be in his bassinet and to stay wrapped in his tight swaddling cloths

throughout his nap. He lay on his side, one tiny fist near his face, the perfect profile of his face softened against the white flannel sheet. So calm, so at peace, so beautiful. Emotion welled up in me. God had given me this precious treasure to love, to care for, to mother through the changes of life. As a new mom, I felt the overwhelming sense of God's creation, His perfect formation of this tiny child in my care.

In this lesson, we'll begin at the beginning. We'll consider who God is as Creator and Father. We'll look at the specifics of how creation was formed and then draw some applications from this.

Part 1

1. Read **Genesis 1:1–2**. How is the earth described in these verses?

2. Read **Genesis 1:3–27**. Fill in the blanks below:

    God created _____ and _____ (vv. 3–5) on the first day.

    On the second day, God created an expanse (sometimes referred to as a "vault"), or the _____ (vv. 6–8).

    God gathered the waters, and then called the dry land _____ and the gathered waters _____ (vv. 9–10). And then on the third day, God said, "Let the earth sprout _____" (v. 11).

    On the fourth day, God created two lights in the sky, the _____ and the _____ (vv. 14–19).

    On the fifth day, God created _____ and _____ (vv. 20–23).

    On the sixth day, God created _____ _____, _____, and _____ (v. 24); and last He created _____ in His own image (vv. 26–28).

3. As you review these verses, what is the repeating refrain? In other words, how is the creation described? (See **vv. 4a, 10b, 12b, 18b, 21b, 25b.**)

Digging Deeper, Part 1

6. How does this knowledge of God as your Creator change the way you think about yourself? This information is likely not new to you, but how does reconsidering these verses give you a renewed sense of purpose?

4. Compare: How did God create the world and living creatures (see **Genesis 1:20–22, 24–25**), and how did He create humans (see **Genesis 2:7, 21–22**)?

7. Even further, how does the fact that God created you *in His own image* change the way you view yourself and your purpose?

5. What is unique about people (see **Genesis 1:26–27**)?

Part 2

8. Why is it that some people do not believe in God as the Creator of the world? (See **Hebrews 11:3**.)

When thinking about the origin of the world, everyone must go on faith. No human was there to observe the formation of the world, of course. Even those who cling to the theory of evolution must rely on their beliefs and not hard scientific data. Instead, Christians, by faith, hold to what the Bible teaches—that God formed everything by His mighty, powerful Word.

9. So, who is God, the One who made all of creation? Let's begin by considering His name. What is the name we call God, our Creator? (See **Malachi 2:10; Matthew 5:9**.)

10. Because of sin, we were separated from God and His perfect creation in the Garden of Eden (**Genesis 3**). This great divide between God and man is described in **Romans 8:7**. Write a summary of it in your own words.

11. What is the reason we can call ourselves children of God? (See **Galatians 3:26–28** and **John 3:16–18**.)

12. Jesus, our "go-between" or mediator, brought us back to God. Read **2 Corinthians 5:19** and **1 John 2:2**. How is Jesus, our mediator, described, and what is His work on our behalf?

13. Another image of God is related in **Isaiah 64:8–9**. How is the relationship between the Lord and His people described in these verses?

Digging Deeper, Part 2

14. You are God's own child, created in His image. What impact does this have on how you live?

15. What impact does the knowledge of being God's own child have on how you treat yourself? how you treat others?

We were made by God's loving, patient, artistic hand. He is the potter; we are the clay. He shaped us into the perfect creation, made in His own image. We see glimpses of this perfect creation in a baby's tiny fingers, though we know this world is tainted by sin. But we trust that God is our Father and we are His children through the sacrifice of Christ on the cross for our salvation. We are adopted into God's kingdom through the washing of Baptism through water and the Word. These biblical truths not only underpin our understanding of creation and the beginning of the world, but they also shape our thoughts and beliefs about our eternal condition. Write a prayer of thanksgiving, with a grateful heart to God for all of His good gifts.

Verse to remember:

By faith we understand that the universe was created by the word of God, so that what is seen was not made out of things that are visible.

Hebrews 11:3

Project: Baby Booties

Skill level: Intermediate

Needles: Set of five US size 5 DPNs; one crochet hook size H or similar size; yarn needle for weaving in ends

Yarn: Bernat Softee Baby or similar weight

Gauge: 2" × 2" 12 stitches and 14 rows in stockinette

Begin with a provisional cast on: With crochet hook, chain five stitches in contrasting scrap yarn of same weight. Slip these loops onto one DPN.

Sole

1. Knit 5 stitches across
2. K1, M1 (make one by knitting in the back of the first stitch, then knit in the front of that stitch; this second knit stitch counts as the next knit stitch, or whatever stitch is needed next), K2, M1, K2 (you should now have 7 stitches)
3. K row
4. K2, M1, K2, M1, K3 (9 stitches)

21

5. K 27 rows
6. K1, K2tog, K3, SSK, K1 (7 stitches)
7. K row
8. K1, K2tog, K1, SSK, K1 (5 stitches)

Sides of foot

1. K 5 across.
2. Pick up and K 16 stitches on side.
3. Remove crochet loops and place 5 stitches on a needle and knit. Pick up and K 16 stitches on side.
4. K around 5 rows.

Top of foot

Work from short end; "SSK" and "P2tog" stitches will be one stitch on working needle and one on the side of the foot.

1. K1, M1, K3, M1, SSK, turn
2. Slip 1 (S1), P5, P2tog, turn
3. S1, M1, K5, M1, SSK, turn
4. S1, P7, P2tog, turn
5. S1, K3, P1, K3, SSK, turn
6. S1, P2, K3, P2, P2tog, turn
7. S1, K1, P5, K1, SSK, turn
8. Repeat row 6
9. Repeat row 5
10. S1, P7, P2tog, turn

Repeat rows 5 through 10 two more times for a total of three repeats.

Cuff

Using the remaining 18 stitches, work in the round.

1. S1 with yarn on the inside of the bootie, K to the end of the round.
2. *K2tog, YO, P2tog, YO. Repeat from * to the end of the round to make eyelets.
3. *K2, P2. Repeat from * to end of the round for a total of 7 rows.

Bind off loosely. Weave in ends.

I-cord

Using one DPN, cast on 2. With another DPN, knit these two stitches, do not turn. Bring the yarn to the back and knit the next row. Repeat until cord measures 14 inches. Weave in ends and thread through eyelet holes. Tie in bow.

Wrapped in God's Love

Several years ago, I saw a sign in front of a florist's shop advertising grave blankets. I didn't know what these would look like—perhaps an array of flowers woven together to look like a blanket, which could then be laid over a grave site. This was new to me, but I immediately understood why it would appeal to the grieving. My grandmother had passed away not long before, and I felt the need, the wish, to somehow protect her, even in death, from the coldness of the earth, the finality of it all. From infancy to the grave, we are wrapped in soft cloth to protect our bodies from the cold, and laying one last blanket over a loved one who has died made perfect sense to me.

When my son was an infant, I got very skilled at swaddling him in blankets. He liked to be tightly wrapped, to feel warmth close to his tiny body. We had one blanket in particular, which was knitted by the hands of a loving woman in our congregation, that even as a young baby he loved. I remember one night in particular, when my husband and I were putting our son to bed in his crib but he cried and cried, and we couldn't figure out what was wrong.

Finally, I covered him with that special blanket, and he calmed right down and fell asleep. That remained his favorite blanket throughout his childhood. He liked the feel of the soft yarn, and he would slip his fingers between the holes woven into the pattern.

When he was three years old, we moved to a new house, and Blankey went missing. Thankfully, we had a backup blanket, but we couldn't figure out where that prized possession could be. I searched high and low, and finally three months later, I found it. A broken hamper had languished in the corner of a guest room, and I finally got around to throwing it out, but first I took a quick peek inside to make sure nothing had been discarded. Sure enough—there was Blankey! Oh! The rejoicing! The happiness! Blankey was found!

Even for adults, we find not only warmth but also comfort in being covered with a blanket. Ever been wrapped in a Snuggie? That's the ultimate in luxurious, comforting warmth. In today's lesson, we will look at some Scripture verses about the metaphorical blanket, or robe, in which Christ clothes us.

These days, we typically do not wear robes except when we climb out of bed and we're not yet dressed. So, for our purposes, robes are a substitute for clothing. However, in Bible times, robes were the common dress. Perhaps this was due to the fact that loose-fitting garments were easier to cut, sew, and finish. Perhaps this was just the style of the day. Whatever the case, a robe can be a garment that is worn around the body to protect us from the cold and to hide our soft flesh.

1. One of the recurring passages of Scripture we'll be discussing during this study is Psalm 139. In this wonderful psalm, we learn about God's unfailing love as our Creator. Read **Psalm 139:13–15**. How would you define the word "knitted" in **verse 13**? Think of your own knitting work or any other work you do with your hands. How would you apply what you know about knitting to this use of the verb in **verse 13**?

2. According to **Psalm 139:13**, how long has God known you? Is this comforting? distressing?

3. If you are a mom, grandmother, aunt, or are in other ways close to kids in your life, think about the long knowledge of their lives that you have. As a mom, for example, you remember your child's first moments outside the womb, the first steps, the first haircut, and so on. Perhaps this is, in a small way, like how God views us. He knows all about us, better than we even know ourselves, perhaps. How do you respond to this understanding of our relationship with God?

4. Read **Job 1:21**. How would you summarize this verse? What does it say about our place in the world?

5. Now let's turn to another Old Testament story, the one about Joseph and his infamous robe of many colors. Joseph was the favored son of Jacob, a patriarch of Israel. It's a tale of intrigue, drama, and great forgiveness. Read **Genesis 37:1–11**. What does Joseph's robe signify to the brothers? Why does this bother them?

6. What do Joseph's brothers do to him? Read **Genesis 37:12–36**.

7. Finally, after many more events occur, Joseph is in a position of power in Egypt and rescues his brothers from the severe famine in the land. Read **Genesis 45:4–15**. What is the overriding theme of this passage?

8. The story of Joseph in the Old Testament is a wonderful picture of the forgiveness Christ has shown to us. Joseph's brothers—guilty of selling their brother into slavery—did not deserve the forgiveness that Joseph gave. But then again, neither do we. Read **Titus 2:14**. Why did Jesus give Himself for us?

9. Now read **Galatians 3:26–27** and **Isaiah 61:10**. Describe how we are clothed.

Digging Deeper

10. Does identifying yourself as God's own child, wrapped in His robe of righteousness, change the way you think of yourself? of others?

11. When you are feeling guilty or down, can this truth bolster your spirits? If so, how?

12. Do you ever struggle with forgiving yourself? Are there times you find this more difficult than others? Why do you think this is so?

13. Are some people or sins easier to forgive than others? Why do you think we want to hold onto grudges? When you struggle with this, what resources or verses could you turn to in order to overcome this?

14. What is one event in the coming week where remembering that you are clothed with Christ's righteousness and love help to give you a better attitude?

Verse to remember:

For as many of you as were baptized into Christ have put on Christ.

Galatians 3:27

Project: Easy Blanket

Skill level: Easy

Needles: US size 6 circular needle at least 24" long; yarn needle for weaving in ends

Yarn: Bernat Softee Baby (5 balls or approximately 1,475 yards) or weight that gives similar gauge

Gauge: 2" × 2" 12 stitches and 14 rows in pattern

Finished size: Approximately 41" × 41"

Cast on 242 stitches

Pattern

Row 1: (K2, P2) repeat to last 2 stitches, K2
Row 2: P2, then K2, P2 across
Row 3: K
Row 4: P
Row 5: Same as row 1
Row 6: Same as row 2
Row 7: P
Row 8: K

When 41" or desired length is reached, bind off.

Option: Cast on 252 stitches. Knit first 5 rows, slipping first stitch as if to purl. Beginning with row 6, knit first 5 stitches. Continue in pattern above to last 5 stitches, then knit last 5 stitches. Continue working blanket to desired length, then knit last 5 rows. This option creates a knitted border that is less likely to roll.

Soggy Babies

Water can be a blessing or a curse. It can rescue or it can drown. We cannot live without water. Our bodies depend on it. Dehydration quickly sets in when we are deprived of water. Extreme stories of survival show just how important water is. With ready access to liquids, we normally feel no deprivation. But just a few hours without water remind us just how much we need this life-giving resource. We also need water to wash, cleanse, and rinse away the things that could hurt our bodies. Without water, crops would fail, and food would also be scarce.

But too much water can be a curse. Flood victims learn this all too well as they see their basements become soggy and possessions ruined by water streaming into their houses. A biblical example of too much water is in the story of Noah and his ark. He rose above the water that destroyed the earth, purifying God's creation. But those who perished in that divine flood felt the true wrath of God and the weight of all that water, drowning and killing them.

A couple of summers ago, I went with my family on a trip to Cape Cod. We took an Amtrak train from Washington DC, past Philadelphia and New York City, through Connecticut and Rhode Island, all the way to Boston. We waited and waited to see the ocean. And then finally, there it was—salt in the air, boats gently rising and falling in the harbor. My husband and I had been to beaches in California and Florida, but never to the Atlantic in New England. A few days after visiting Boston sites, we went to our vacation spot in Cape Cod and headed to the beach.

We tucked ourselves into a postage-stamp area on towels borrowed from the bed-and-breakfast, between all of the other beach visitors. Once settled, we watched the tide coming in. A barge in the distance. A sailboat along the horizon.

But in the foreground, the tide was inching nearer and nearer. These were not the calm, mellow lapping waves of the southern California seashore. These were crashing, foaming, thunderous waves. They felt angry and powerful. Also, signs warning of dangerous riptides dotted the shore. But we were on vacation on the beach. So, I made my way down to the shore and stepped in.

The temperature of the water was numbing. This was not bathwater warm. This was sprinkler cold. But I persevered. I went in up to my waist. Just as I was getting my skin used to the freezing water, suddenly, a wave crashed over me. It tossed me underwater. I felt the tug of the ocean, the weight of the water, the power of the sea as another wave crashed over my head. It rolled me in the sand, pulling me under. It felt like hours went by—a lifetime.

But finally, I came up to air, sputtering and spitting out the bitter seawater. The lifeguards barely glanced my way. My son, who was also in the water, helped me to our towels. I recovered my breath, warmed up in a sweatshirt, and have never doubted the strength of the ocean again.

Water is a powerful force of nature. It can give life and it can destroy. And this is what Baptism does for us too. It gives life and destroys sin. The teaching of Baptism is one of the central doctrines of the Bible, yet it's probably not something we often think about. Baptism is not something that happens to us as an infant that we then can forget about for the rest of our life. Baptism is a gift that keeps on giving. It is a daily, renewing gift that can help us not only to trust in God's forgiveness and love for us at one time—the time of our Baptism—but also to remember that God cherishes and loves us day by day. This session is all about water and the washing—the spiritual washing—that water gives through Baptism. Studying the blessings of Baptism helps us understand the great reassurance and the hope it can give.

If your group chooses to do so, you could make the knitted shell blankets featured in this lesson to give to families with newly baptized babies. Or you may choose another recipient. Either way, let the blessings of Baptism wash over you as you review this important gift of God.

Let's turn to Scripture to highlight some of the important verses that help us understand the teaching of Baptism.

1. What is Baptism? Read **Mark 16:16** and **John 3:5** and describe Baptism in your own words.

2. In other words, what is the purpose of Baptism?

3. Baptism a gift of God, not something we do for God. What is given in this Sacrament?

4. Read **1 Peter 3:18–22**. These verses compare the story of Noah's ark and the flood to Baptism. Read the verses and then think about how these two events could be similar or different. See the events of Noah and the flood in **Genesis 6:9–9:17**. Write your ideas on the next page:

Luther wrote: "Now baptism is by far a greater flood than was that of Noah.... Baptism drowns all sorts of men throughout the world, from the birth of Christ even till the day of judgment.... [Noah's flood] was a flood of wrath, this is a flood of grace" (AE 35:32)

A comparison between Noah's flood and Baptism (add your ideas to the columns below):

Noah's flood	Baptism
element: water	element: water
washed away sin	washes away sin
flood of wrath	flood of grace
God rescued the righteous	God rescues us and pronounces us righteous
God saved	God saves

5. Another Bible story that shows a believer's progression from learning God's Word to a desire for Baptism is the account of Philip and the Ethiopian eunuch. Read **Acts 8:26–30**. When Philip found him, what was the Ethiopian doing?

6. When Philip asked the Ethiopian about whether he understood what he was reading, what was his answer? Read **Acts 8:31**.

7. Since this story features an Ethiopian, someone from a country in Africa, it could represent for us the fact that God was opening His kingdom to people outside Israel. The gifts of Baptism extend to all people, not only to the chosen few. Read **Acts 2:38–39** and **Mark 10:13–15**. To whom does the kingdom belong, according to these verses?

Digging Deeper

8. Often, one tradition that is maintained in congregations is to use a scallop shell to pour the water over the baptized. The origin of this tradition is not known. It is speculated that John the Baptist used a shell to baptize Jesus, but this is not in the scriptural record. Often, in church art, a shell might be shown with three drops of water below it. What do you think these three drops of water might symbolize? Why might this be associated with Baptism? (See **Matthew 28:19**.)

9. What are some special traditions you have for the newly baptized, either in your congregation or in your family? Do these traditions help you to remain more connected to the blessings of your Baptism?

10. What is your Baptism birthday? Write it here: _____. If you do not know it, try to track down the day so you can celebrate this as God's own child.

Verse to remember:

Baptism... now saves you, not as a removal of dirt from the body but as an appeal to God for a good conscience.

1 Peter 3:21

Project: Shell-Stitch Blanket

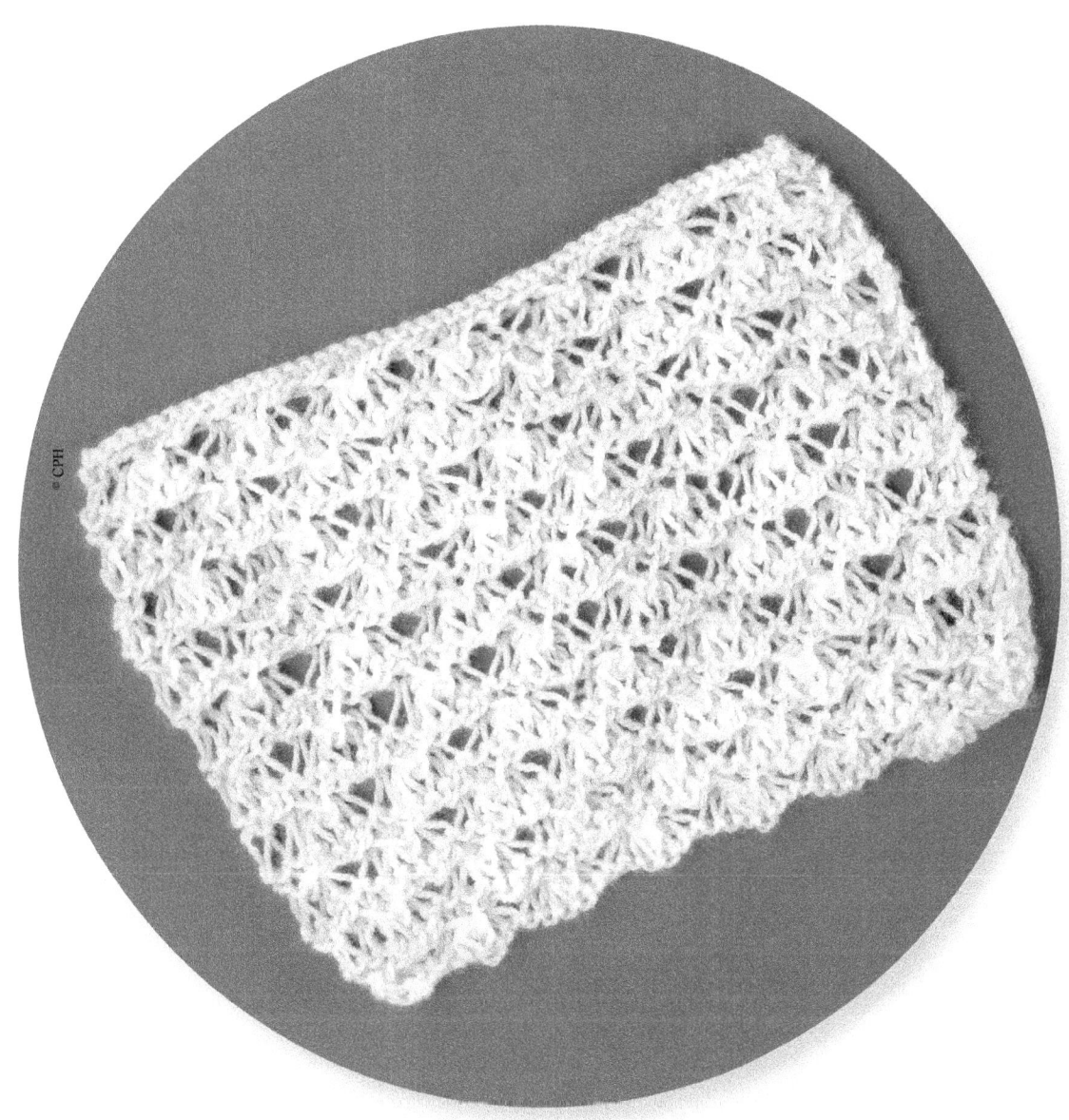

Skill level: Experienced

Needles: US size 6 circular needle at least 24" long; yarn needle for weaving in ends

Yarn: Bernat Softee Baby (4 balls or approximately 1,200 yards) or weight that gives similar gauge

Gauge: 2" × 2" 12 stitches and 8 rows in pattern

Finished size: Approximately 40" × 40"

Cast on 183 stitches and work until blanket is 40" long or desired length. Knit very loosely or this pattern will be difficult to knit.

Cast on 183 stitches and work until blanket is 40" long or desired length. Knit very loosely or this pattern will be difficult to knit.

Pattern

Row 1: K1, (YO, K1) across, end K1

Row 2: K across but do not knit YO stitches from last row; rather, drop these stitches and K only K stitches

Row 3: K1, K3tog, (YO2 ×, K1, YO2 ×, slip 2 purlwise, K3tog and P2SSO) across until 5 stitches remain, then YO2 ×, K1, YO2 ×, K3tog, K1. Note: for P2SSO, you must pass both slipped stitches over the one stitch remaining after the K3tog

Row 4: K1, (K1, K1 in front of 1st YO, K1 in back of 2nd YO) until 2 stitches remain, K2

Row 5: Same as row 1

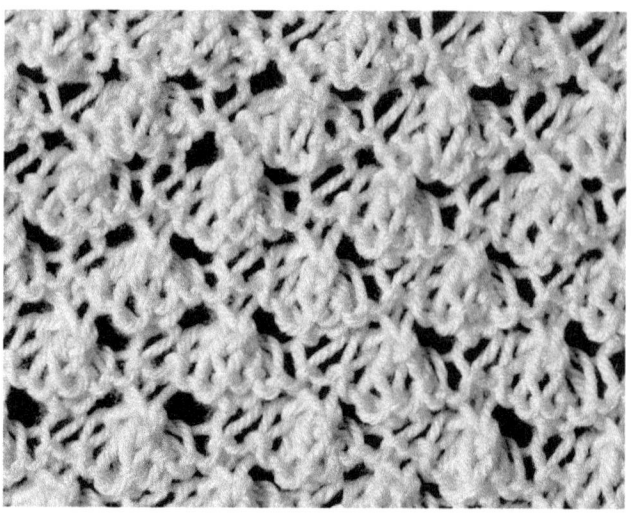

Row 6: Same as row 2

Row 7: K1, (K1, YO2, slip 2 purlwise, k3tog and P2SSO, YO2) until 2 stitches remain, K2

Row 8: Same as row 4

Continue knitting until blanket is desired length, approximately 40", then knit last 2 rows. Bind off very loosely. Weave in ends.

Life to the Fullest

Lambs, sheep, and shepherds are mentioned in the Bible over five hundred times, more than any other animal. Do some of your favorite passages of Scripture discuss sheep? They just may. "The Lord is my shepherd" is from Psalm 23. "My sheep listen to My voice; I know them, and they follow Me" is from John 10. What was young David's occupation? Shepherd. Which animal did Jesus say He would search out and find? A lost lamb. Who were some of the first people to see the infant Savior? Shepherds. What is a favorite name of Jesus? The Lamb of God. The Bible is full of bleating, woolly sheep.

Why is this? Why is God's Word full of these woolly critters? While our interaction with sheep may be limited to petting zoos and children's books, the ancient Israelites would have been well familiar with sheep and their habits and behaviors. The ancient Israelites depended on "portable" livestock, like sheep, in their nomadic existence. Having many flocks and herds was a symbol of wealth. The bigger your flocks and herds, the richer you were—sort of like driving around a Hummer or BMW or owning a mansion would shout success today. The Israelites used the milk and meat of sheep for food, they used the wool and skins for clothing, and they offered them as sacrifices.

So, God, who is always coming to us, speaking to us in our own language, spoke to the Israelites about sheep. But we non-nomadic people may need to learn a bit about sheep, lambs, and shepherds in order to become better versed in biblical language.

For a city dweller, like me, the idea of farming and raising livestock seems like a grand adventure. But when I actually do any research, I realize that farming is extremely hard work—and beyond the stamina of this city girl. Nevertheless, a couple of years ago, I had the brilliant idea that I wanted to own alpacas.

At the time, I was in an intense knitting phase. I decided that I wanted to keep alpacas, shear them, spin their fleece into yarn, and make fabulous sweaters. I still love them and will attend the occasional alpaca festival, just for fun (weirdo that I am). But I'm not sure I'm cut out for all of the hard physical labor of a farm. You don't get a day off. There's no sleeping in—those animals are hungry! Your shoes get smeared with manure. You have to tend to the critters, maintain fences, clean out stalls, and do a multitude of other tasks.

I love the *All Creatures Great and Small* books, and recently, I started watching the TV episodes of this old show on DVD. James Herriot, the pen name of James Wight, was an author who chronicled his experiences as a country veterinarian in England (jamesherriot.org/life-and-times). The stories of his work in the mud and muck of barns and fields among the animals in the English countryside do not glamorize the work, but rather show how "down and dirty" a country vet must get in order to keep animals healthy and well. He deals with nasty-sounding conditions, such as sheep mange and foot rot. He births the lambs and calves and puts his fist in places it definitely should not be.

As I researched information on sheep and lambs, I found some interesting facts. Did you know that wet sheep smell like wet wool? An adult female is called a ewe, a male is a ram, and a young sheep is a lamb. Mutton is meat from sheep; lamb comes from the young. But you do *not* want to know what lamb fries are! Trust me.

So what does all this sheep talk have to do with you living a fulfilling life? Plenty. Let's dive into Scripture to see if we can find out a bit more about these woolly creatures.

1. In John 10, Jesus compares Himself to a shepherd and His followers to sheep. Read **John 10:1–5**. Describe the relationship between the sheep and the shepherd.

2. More specifically, *how* does the shepherd lead the sheep (**vv. 4–5**)?

3. In the Middle East, shepherds lead their sheep differently than in the West. Ranchers in the U.S. may drive their flocks from behind, pushing them along. But in the Middle East, shepherds lead in the front. Their voice bids the sheep and lambs to follow. Read **John 10:3** again and **Romans 10:17**. How does this compare to how God leads His people?

4. Sheep are not known as being the most intelligent of animals. In fact, they are usually considered rather stupid. However, they know at least one thing. Read **verses 4 and 5** again. What is it that sheep recognize?

Digging Deeper

Sheep realize that their shepherd knows what's best; they will stay close to him and not doubt his care. If they get in trouble, they bleat for their shepherd. When it's dark and the wolves are howling, they know that to stay safe, they must stick close by their shepherd. Sheep know they are weak and helpless without their shepherd.

In the same way, we as God's sheep should remain close to our Shepherd, Jesus. We go where He is. We listen to His voice. We stay safe. But the problem is that we don't realize our need for our Shepherd. We don't see ourselves as weak or helpless. We are strong, confident, fierce women of God, right? If we truly realized how weak and helpless we are without God as our Shepherd, we would flee to Him at all times. We would not wander off.

While we may have our moments of strength, we often cannot handle how hectic our days are. We get frustrated with the people around us. We have headaches and migraines and stomachaches that remind us how weak we truly are. We feel guilt for things we have neglected to do or things we have done wrong. We worry excessively about our children and their choices in life. We get overwhelmed easily.

5. Describe a time when you felt this sense of weakness or helplessness and you cried out to God. What led you to that point? What came of the experience?

6. Read **John 10:10–15**. Describe the difference between a hired hand and a good shepherd from these verses.

7. How does Jesus define what a good shepherd does in **verses 14–15**?

8. Luther wrote: "In this single little word 'shepherd' there are gathered together in one almost all the good and comforting things that we praise in God" (AE 12:152). A bad shepherd (or hired hand) abandons the sheep when they most need him. A good shepherd, however, goes to extreme lengths—even by laying down his life—to protect and care for the sheep. Read **John 10:17–18**. Why did Christ, our Good Shepherd, lay down His life?

9. As you close your Bible study today, read aloud **Psalm 23**. Choose one verse that is the most meaningful to you and challenge yourself to memorize it this week. Why did you choose this verse?

Verse to remember:

The thief comes only to steal and kill and destroy. I came that they may have life and have it abundantly.

John 10:10

Project: Sheep Toy

Skill level: Experienced

Needles: Set of five or six US size 8 DPNs (longer needles recommended); yarn needle for weaving in ends

Yarn: Medium weight, such as Vanna's Choice by Lion brand, one ball each of white and taupe (suggested colors)

Other: Fiberfill stuffing

Gauge: Not applicable

Finished size: Approximately 8½" tall

Directions *for fur loop stitch*

Row 1: K1 but do not drop stitch from left needle. Bring yarn to the front of the work. Wind the yarn around the left thumb and bring the yarn into the back of the work. Knit the same stitch you knit before and let it drop. YO front to back. Pass the last 2 stitches (ones just created) over the yarn over as for binding off. Withdraw thumb from the loop. Repeat to the end of the row.

Row 2: Knit

Body

Cast on 21 stitches. Distribute evenly or close to evenly on needles and join in the round, being careful to not twist stitches.

Knit 1 row.

Purl 1 row.

Fur Stitch 1: (1 pattern row, 1 knit row)

Fur Stitch 2: (1 pattern row, 1 knit row in which you increase 3 stitches by knitting into the front and back of a stitch—evenly spaced—for 24 stitches total)

Fur Stitch 3: (1 pattern row, 1 knit row in which you increase 6 stitches by knitting into the front and back of a stitch—evenly spaced—for 30 stitches total)

Fur Stitch 4: (1 pattern row, 1 knit row)

Fur Stitch 5: (1 pattern row, 1 knit row in which you increase 10 stitches by knitting into the front and back of a stitch—evenly spaced—for 40 stitches total)

Fur Stitch 6–8: (1 pattern row, 1 knit row)

Fur Stitch 9: (1 pattern row, 1 knit row in which you decrease 10 stitches by knitting 2 together—evenly spaced in the round—for 30 stitches total)

Fur Stitch 10: (1 pattern row, 1 knit row in which you decrease 10 stitches by knitting 2 together—evenly spaced in the round—for 20 stitches total)

Fur Stitch 11: (1 pattern row, 1 knit row in which you decrease 6 stitches by knitting 2 together—evenly spaced in the round—for 14 stitches total)

Fur Stitch 12: (1 pattern row, 1 knit row in which you decrease 7 stitches by knitting 2 together—evenly spaced in the round—for 7 stitches total)

Knit one round.

Cut yarn, leaving a 6" tail. Slip tail through all stitches and fasten off.

Head

Cast on 21 stitches and join in the round, distributing stitches evenly and being careful not to twist.

Knit 1 row in the round.

Fur Stitch 1 round and K one round, increasing 7 stitches in this round.

Complete another Fur Stitch row and K stitch pair of rows.

Back of head

You will be using 14 stitches for the back of the head; remaining stitches are held in reserve on needles until you make the face.

S1 Fur Stitch across, K last stitch, turn.

S1 Purl to end, turn.

Repeat these last 2 rows 4 times, ending with a purl row.

Top of head

Row 1: K1, Fur Stitch 7, SSK, turn.

Row 2: S1, P2, P2tog, turn.

Knit Row: S1, Fur Stitch to within 1 of gap, SSK, turn.

Purl Row: S1, P to within 1 of gap, P2tog, turn.

Repeat these last 2 rows until no gap stitches remain and there are 4 stitches on the needle.

Face

Using contrasting color:

Row 1: K across 4 stitches on needle, pick up and K5. K across reserved 14 stitches. Pick up and K5 and transfer 2 stitches from needle 1. There should be 7 stitches on needles 1 and 3, and 14 stitches on needle 2.

Row 2: K across needle 1 until 1 stitch remains. K this last stitch together (K2tog) with the first stitch on needle 2; leave on needle 1, turn.

Row 3: S1, P across needles 1 and 3 until 1 stitch remains. P this last stitch together (P2tog) with the last stitch on needle 2; keep on needle 3, turn.

Row 4: S1, K across needles 1 and 3 until 1 stitch remains. K this last stitch together (K2tog) with the first stitch on needle 2; leave on needle 1, turn.

Repeat rows 3 and 4 until 4 stitches remain on needle 2.

S1 on first round only and then K around for 5 rows.

Next row: (K1, K2tog) repeat around.

Next row: K around.

Next row: K2tog around.

Cut yarn, leaving a 6" tail. Slip tail through all stitches and fasten off.

Ear (make 2)

Cast on 5.

Row 1: P

Row 2: K

Row 3: P

Row 4: K2tog, K1, SSK

Row 5: P

Bind off. Cut yarn, leaving a 6" tail.

Leg (make 4)

Cast on 8 using one DPN.

With another DPN, K across. Do not turn.

K across again, bringing yarn across the back of the needle and pulling tight. This will make a closed loop/tube of knitting.

Repeat until leg is 2 inches long.

Cut yarn, leaving a 6" tail. Slip tail through all stitches and fasten off.

Tail

Cast on 5.
Row 1: P
Row 2: K
Row 3: P
Row 4: K
Row 5: P
Row 6: K
Row 7: P
Row 8: K2tog, K1, SSK
Bind off. Cut yarn, leaving a 6" tail.

Assembly

Use fiberfill to stuff body and head to desired shape and consistency so sheep sits by itself. With yarn needle, attach head to body first, matching holes to form neck. Sew on ears, legs, and tail. With white yarn, embroider eyes. Use ends of yarn wherever possible to assemble. Finally, weave in ends and cut yarn.

Shelter from the Storm

Storm Chasers is a TV show on the Discovery Channel that follows severe storms in the spring months when tornado season is at its most active. The "chasers" are scientists trying to capture the most intense, destructive tornadoes and storms that threaten towns and cities in the U.S. "tornado alley." The scientists' goal is to gain as much information as possible about these storms in order to help in the future with early notification for residents to try to prevent loss of life when tornadoes strike.

So, while everyone in town is seeking shelter or trying to outrun the approaching storms, these guys head straight into the worst of it. The teams take ordinary cars and turn them into tanks that can survive damaging hail and even a tornado. Some of the footage these researchers capture includes funnel clouds stretching down from the sky, widening, and then becoming gray and brown as they circulate dirt and debris from the ground it into the sky.

So what are the major storms that arise in your life? For some, marriage is a thorny and difficult issue. Couples struggle financially or are unhappy with work or . . . The list could go on and on, and all of those struggles can cause strife in marriage.

Divorce can cause not only many complications and emotional difficulties, but also financial troubles.

The children struggle too, and in the middle of the storm is mom, herself grieving over a loss and dealing with the headaches of daily life without a partner.

Dealing with the death of a family member or friend can cause major storms in our lives. A parent dying causes much grief and a feeling of being "lost" in the world. Also, it is said that the most difficult storm that a couple can weather is the death of a child.

A storm that I faced earlier in my married life was the challenge of secondary infertility. Our son was born in 1995. We didn't realize it at the time, but he was our "miracle baby." We hoped for more children, so when our son was around three years old, we made the decision to try, but those children never came. My husband and I sought medical help, but after surgeries and medicines and treatment, each month came along like a mini funeral. My concerned friends decided they'd try to avoid talking about babies and pregnancies, but it was awkward and difficult because they were all having more children while our only child approached kindergarten.

Finally, after years of struggling, we decided to stop treatment and let the size of our family be determined by what we already had. Looking back now, years later, I can see God's care and protection during this storm in my life. I cried through the pain. I talked incessantly about it, telling my friends about the struggles. I couldn't shut up. The desire to be a mom, whether for one child or more, had me on my knees, begging God for another baby. I had imagined my two-to-three child household bustling with activity and music and children playing and laughing. But it was not to be.

It's been many years since those days when our son was so small. There will always be a part of me that mourns the loss of more children. As a mom, I've had only one of all of the experiences and milestones you expect in parenthood: one first step, one kindergarten graduation, one confirmation. And yet, even though I still get those pangs of disappointment, I give thanks for all the blessings God has poured out on me and my family.

The point is that there *will* be storms along life's way. We will have losses and disappointments. Pain and suffering, sadly, are part of our earthly experience. But how will we react when those difficulties arise? Will we fall apart? Will we bounce back with grace and courage?

Psalm 91 is one of many psalms of reassurance and hope. There are certain passages of Scripture that are like a pool of light in a darkened room. We let these words soak in during the dark and difficult times of our lives. Psalm 91 is one of these passages.

1. Read **Psalm 91:1–2**. Four specific words stand out in these verses. They are noted below. Answer two questions about each: (a) describe what the item is; (b) describe how God could be compared to each.

   a. Shelter, what:

   b. Shelter, how:

2. a. Shadow, what:

   b. Shadow, how:

3. a. Refuge, what:

   b. Refuge, how:

4. a. Fortress, what:

   b. Fortress, how:

5. Read **Psalm 91:3–4**. These verses use language that might be unfamiliar to some.
   - The "snare of a fowler" is any type of trap that entangles or captures a bird. "Entangle" immediately brings up the

image of a bird caught in a web of cords. The more it struggles, the more deeply is it caught in the tangle.

- "Pestilence" is more familiar. It is a plague or any kind of evil or destruction.
- "Pinions" are feathers or parts of a wing.
- "Shield and buckler" are very similar in meaning. A "buckler" is a type of round shield—usually worn with a strap around the arm—used for defense or protection.

Now, knowing the definitions of these words, how would you summarize these two verses?

6. Continue by reading **Psalm 91:5–10**. One thing that stands out in this psalm is the imagery and visual description. Read these verses and let the images wash over you. Picture yourself as the one walking, completely protected in the hands of God, as "a thousand . . . fall at your side" and the "pestilence" stalks everyone but you. What thoughts and feelings come to mind as you read these verses and picture yourself in the midst of these images?

7. Psalm 91 tells of God's abiding protection and care as well as an important characteristic of the child of God. Read **Psalm 31:14** and **Psalm 37:5** and describe what this quality is.

8. Read **Hebrews 11:1**. What is another word for this quality? How does this quality characterize the believer and his or her attitude?

9. Read **Ephesians 2:8–9** and **1 Corinthians 12:3**. These verses describe the Holy Spirit's work in our lives. What does the Spirit create within us? Why do we need Him to do so?

10. The next verses of Psalm 91 describe the work of the angels. Read **Psalm 103:20–21** and **Psalm 91:11–12**. Satan used these words to tempt Jesus (see **Matthew 4:6**). He twists the reassurance of these verses into a temptation for Jesus to throw Himself off a high cliff and test God's care. Satan often tries to tempt us by twisting what is good into something sinful. How do God's Word and the angels help us?

13. After reading these verses, what could you share with a friend to help when storms of life descend upon him or her?

Digging Deeper

11. What comfort do you find in God's words in Psalm 91:14–16?

14. Consider the role of faith and trust in your life. Is it easy for you to trust in God? Difficult? What are some barriers that you could break down in order to make your faith grow?

12. As you have now meditated on the loving protection of God throughout the verses of Psalm 91, what are some actions you could take during the storms in your life to help you recall and remember God's love and care?

God's loving protection shelters and encircles those who trust in Him, as is so beautifully described in Psalm 91. While we sometimes struggle amid the snares and tangles of life, we can rest assured that our heavenly Father cares for us and will see us through every storm and difficulty and help us to move through our days with grace as we trust in Him.

Beyond the storms of this life, God has promised us eternal shelter under His wings, as we read in Revelation 7:15: "Therefore they are before the throne of God, and serve Him day and night in His temple; and He who sits on the throne will shelter them with His presence." So, bring it on, storms! Let's hear the thunder growl and see the lightning flash. We have a God whose care will never fail or falter.

Verse to remember:

He who dwells in the shelter of the Most High will abide in the shadow of the Almighty. I will say to the LORD, "My refuge and my fortress, my God, in whom I trust."

Psalm 91:1–2

Project: Easy Hat

Skill level: Easy if made without the trim edge, stripes, and pompon; otherwise, medium difficulty

Needles: Set of five or six US size 5 DPNs; US size 4 straight needles for the trim edge; yarn needle for weaving in ends and for optional pompon

Yarn: Bernat Softee Baby or weight that gives similar gauge, plus contrasting yarn of similar weight for optional trim edge, if desired

Gauge: 2" × 2" 14 stitches and 14 rows in pattern

Finished size: 10" circumference when relaxed. The ribbing makes this hat very stretchy.

For optional trim edge

Cast on 80 stitches, using straight needles. (Can be done in a contrasting color from the body of hat.)

Rows 1–3: K

Row 4: *K4, twist right needle completely around. Repeat from * until there are four stitches left. K last four stitches.

Row 5: Switch to DPN. Divide stitches evenly over four or five DPNs. Place marker. Join in the round, being careful not to twist. Continue with pattern as below.

Body

If no trim was made, cast on 80 stitches and divide evenly over four or five DPNs. Place marker. Join, being careful not to twist. Continue in pattern.

Pattern: *K2, P2. Repeat from * to end of row. Continue knitting until hat is 4" long.

Decrease for crown

Row 1: *K2, P2tog. Repeat from * to end.
Rows 2–4: K2, P1 all the way around.
Row 5: *K2tog, P1. Repeat from * to end.
Rows 6–7: K1, P1 all the way around.
Row 8: *K2tog, P2tog. Repeat from * to end.
Row 9: K1, P1 all the way around.
Row 10: K2tog all the way around.

Cut yarn and use a yarn needle to thread yarn end through remaining stitches on needles; fasten off.

Optional pompon

Use a 1"-wide ruler (wooden preferred) or stiff card stock. Wrap yarn around ruler or card stock 60–70 times. Cut yarn. Thread a doubled length of yarn on a heavyweight sewing needle and sew all layers of yarn at the middle on both sides of the ruler or card stock. When yarn is secure, slip it off the ruler or card stock. Wrap yarn tightly around the middle of the pompom (where you've sewn the layers together). Cut each end of the yarn loops, opposite from where you sewed them together. Trim ends so they are even, and sew the pompon to the top of the hat. Fluff yarn so it makes a ball.

Pattern option

Make stripes by using contrasting yarn. Suggested color placement: After trim, knit 1½ inches, then change color. Knit three rows of each color, carrying yarn on the wrong side. When hat is desired length, break second color and weave in ends. Continue with main color to end.

The Ordinary and the Extraordinary

Session 6

A few years ago, I volunteered to work on the altar guild at our church, something I'd never done before. I knew these faithful women set out the flower arrangements that adorned the altar, set up for Communion, cleaned the linens, and took care of other practical needs of the altar. But that's about all I knew about their work. So, when I started, all of the particulars of our altar guild confused me. There was a set of silver for early service and another one for late service. I was supposed to count out the wafers and place them on the "paten" and then use the "ciborium" for some other purpose. It was all strange and different—a new, secret churchy language. But all of this I expected to learn. As a pastor's wife, I'd heard some of these terms before and expected to get better acquainted with them as I learned the ropes of the altar guild.

What I didn't expect was to learn just how ordinary the elements used in Communion are. The wine we use for Communion is not flown in from the Mount of Olives in Israel. It isn't special wine blessed by a bishop somewhere. It is ordinary white wine that comes in a one-gallon green jug with a screw-top cap. At first, this was a little disconcerting. I sort of wanted my Communion wine to seem special in some way. But then I realized that this isn't what is important.

55

I learned that it's not the quality of the grape or the type of wine used in Communion that changed the essential meaning of the Sacrament. The wine could be red or white, a Bordeaux or a chardonnay. It could come in a gallon jug or a crystal bottle. None of this added importance or meaning to Communion. I learned anew that what is important is God's Word attached to this ordinary wine. That is what gives it its power.

A friend recently told me about an upcoming Baptism at her church. A worker at her church had recently made a trip to Israel and had brought home a bottle of water from the Jordan River. She said that from her bottle, she would be adding three drops of water to the baptismal font for each Baptism until it was all gone.

My first thought was *Wow—how neat to have your baby baptized with water from the Jordan River!* That was where Jesus was baptized, after all.

My second thought was *Well, doesn't God sanctify* all *water used in Baptism? Couldn't regular city tap water be used? Did adding water from the Jordan River make a Baptism better in some way?*

On the one hand, yes, having water from the Jordan attached some symbolic meaning to the Sacrament. But on the other hand, what is really the power of Baptism is the Word of God attached to that water—wherever that water may have come from. We sometimes add sentimental or symbolic meaning to spiritual things, and that's completely fine. Symbols can help us understand and connect to God's Word. We wear crosses on our necklaces and color our churches with beautiful stained glass depicting doves and lambs. Understanding those symbols can help us remember the meaning of God's Word and its importance in our lives. We use music and art and symbols in order to help communicate the Gospel, which is good.

The danger is that attaching superstitious meaning to symbols could distract from the true meaning of Baptism or the Lord's Supper. The true meaning of the Sacraments comes from God's Word attached to the ordinary element. A Baptism performed with Jordan River water is not more powerful than a Baptism performed with regular tap water. There is not more grace given to the newly baptized dipped in the Jordan as opposed to a baby whose head is sprinkled with city tap water in Minnesota.

1. So in considering what Baptism is and the benefits of it, let's look at some Bible verses. As Luther asks in his Small Catechism, how can water in Baptism do such great things? Read **Titus 3:5–8** and **Ephesians 5:26**.

2. What are the "great things" that Baptism does for us?

3. Read **Matthew 26:28**. Why is Jesus' blood "poured out," according to this verse?

4. What are the benefits of the Lord's Supper? Read **1 John 1:7** and **1 Peter 2:24** and describe these benefits.

5. Read **Hebrews 9:19–25**. According to verse 22, what is necessary for forgiveness?

6. Jesus forgives us, removes our sins, and restores us in our relationship to God. This forgiveness is applied to us in the Sacraments of Baptism and the Lord's Supper. God uses humble means to perform miracles. Read **Ephesians 1:7**. How do we have this forgiveness?

What makes the Sacrament efficacious, or effective, is God's Word. It's God's living Word that gives the power to these ordinary elements in order to bring about a spiritual miracle—to grant us salvation, forgiveness, and eternal life.

God takes ordinary things, like water, bread, and wine and elevates them by combining them with His Word. It's not the water that matters but the water combined with the power of God's Word that brings about salvation for the baptized. It's not the wine or bread that matters, but the words spoken that combine these ordinary elements with the extraordinary benefits from God's Word.

God uses the ordinary to do extraordinary things. Ordinary water works with the Word to regenerate sinners. Bread and wine works with the Word to forgive the repentant.

Digging Deeper

7. God also uses ordinary people to do extraordinary things. Read **2 Corinthians 4:6–7**. How do these verses describe where God places the "treasure" He gives? Why does this language seem fitting?

8. What is the "treasure" God places in these humble "jars of clay"?

9. What is the context of St. Paul's meaning? Why does he refer to himself as a "jar of clay"?

10. Similarly, we also are the "temple" of God (2 Corinthians 6:16). We are vessels that hold this great treasure—God's Holy Spirit. What is Paul saying about the "temple of the living God"?

11. We are ordinary believers, trusting in God's mercy as His disciples. But God takes the ordinary and does extraordinary things. How does God use you to do these extraordinary things?

12. How might God continue to use your gifts to do extraordinary things in His kingdom in the future?

The source of the water used in the font or the kind of wine used in Communion is not as significant as the powerful Word of God. God's Word gives Baptism power. God's Word gives the Lord's Supper its forgiving properties.

Likewise, it was not the wood of the cross that mattered. It was the body hanging there. It was Jesus, bloodied and broken on the cross, who gave us what we needed—forgiveness and reconciliation with the Father. And for this, we take our ordinary lives and use them for His extraordinary purposes.

Verse to remember:

Looking to Jesus, the founder and perfecter of our faith, who for the joy that was set before Him endured the cross, despising the shame, and is seated at the right hand of the throne of God.

Hebrews 12:2

Project: Baptism Shell Washcloth

Skill level: Easy

Needles: US size 5 straight needles; yarn needle for weaving in ends

Yarn: Cotton, such as Lily's Sugar and Cream, or weight that gives similar gauge

Gauge: 2" × 2" 9 stitches and 13 rows in pattern

Finished size: Approximately 8" × 8"

Cast on 36 inches. Slip the first stitch of every row purl wise.

Follow the chart. On the right side, knit the blank squares and purl the marked squares. On the wrong side, purl the blank squares and knit the marked squares.

Row 1 Cast on 46 stitches

Row 2 K

Row 3 K

Row 4 K

Row 5 K5, P36, K5

Row 6 K

Row 7 K5, P36, K5

Row 8 K

Row 9 K5, P36, K5

Row 10	K18, P10, K to end of row
Row 11	K5, P12, K12, P12, K5
Row 12	K17, P14, K to end
Row 13	K5, P11, K14, P11, K5
Row 14	K16, P12, K to end
Row 15	K5, P12, K12, P12, K5
Row 16	K18, P10, K to end
Row 17	K5, P13, K10, P13, K5
Row 18	K17, P2, K1, P1, K1, P2, K1, P1, K1, P2, K17
Row 19	K5, P11, K3, P1, K1, P1, K2, P1, K1, P1, K3, P11, K5
Row 20	K15, P3, K1, P2, K1, P2, K1, P2, K1, P3, K15
Row 21	K5, P10, K3, P1, K2, P1, K2, P1, K2, P1, K3, P10, K5
Row 22	K14, P4, K1, P2, K1, P2, K1, P2, K1, P4, K14
Row 23	K5, P9, K3, P2, K2, P1, K2, P1, K2, P2, K3, P9, K5
Row 24	K13, P4, K1, P2, K2, P2, K2, P2, K1, P4, K13
Row 25	K5, P7, K4, P2, K2, P1, K4, P1, K2, P2, K4, P7, K5
Row 26	K12, P4, K1, P3, K1, P4, K1, P3, K1, P4, K12
Row 27	K5, P6, K5, P1, K3, P1, K4, P1, K3, P1, K5, P6, K5
Row 28	K11, P5, K1, P3, K1, P4, K1, P3, K1, P5, K11
Row 29	K5, P5, K5, P2, K3, P1, K4, P1, K3, P2, K5, P5, K5
Row 30	K10, P5, K1, P4, K1, P4, K1, P4, K1, P5, K10
Row 31	K5, P4, K6, P1, K3, P2, K4, P2, K3, P1, K6, P4, K5
Row 32	K9, P5, K2, P3, K1, P6, K1, P3, K2, P5, K9
Row 33	K5, P3, K6, P1, K4, P1, K6, P1, K4, P1, K6, P3, K5
Row 34	K8, P6, K1, P4, K1, P6, K1, P4, K1, P6, K8
Row 35	K5, P3, K5, P2, K4, P1, K6, P1, K4, P2, K5, P3, K5
Row 36	K8, P5, K1, P5, K1, P6, K1, P5, K1, P5, K8
Row 37	K5, P3, K5, P1, K4, P2, K6, P2, K4, P1, K5, P3, K5

Row 38	K8, P4, K2, P4, K1, P8, K1, P4, K2, P4, K8
Row 39	K5, P4, K2, P2, K5, P1, K8, P1, K5, P2, K2, P4, K5
Row 40	K12, P6, K1, P8, K1, P6, K12
Row 41	K5, P6, K6, P2, K8, P2, K6, P6, K5
Row 42	K11, P6, K1, P10, K1, P6, K11
Row 43	K5, P7, K5, P1, K10, P1, K5, P7, K5
Row 44	K13, P4, K1, P10, K1, P4, K13
Row 45	K5, P9, K2, P2, K10, P2, K2, P9, K5
Row 46	K17, P12, K17
Row 47	K5, P12, K12, P12, K5
Row 48	K18, P10, K18
Row 49	K5, P14, K8, P14, K5
Row 50	K21, P4, K21

Row 51 K5, P36, K5

Row 52 K

Row 53 K5, P36, K5

Row 54 K

Row 55 K5, P36, K5

Row 56 K

Row 57 K

Row 58 K

Bind off loosely.

Cut yarn and weave in ends.

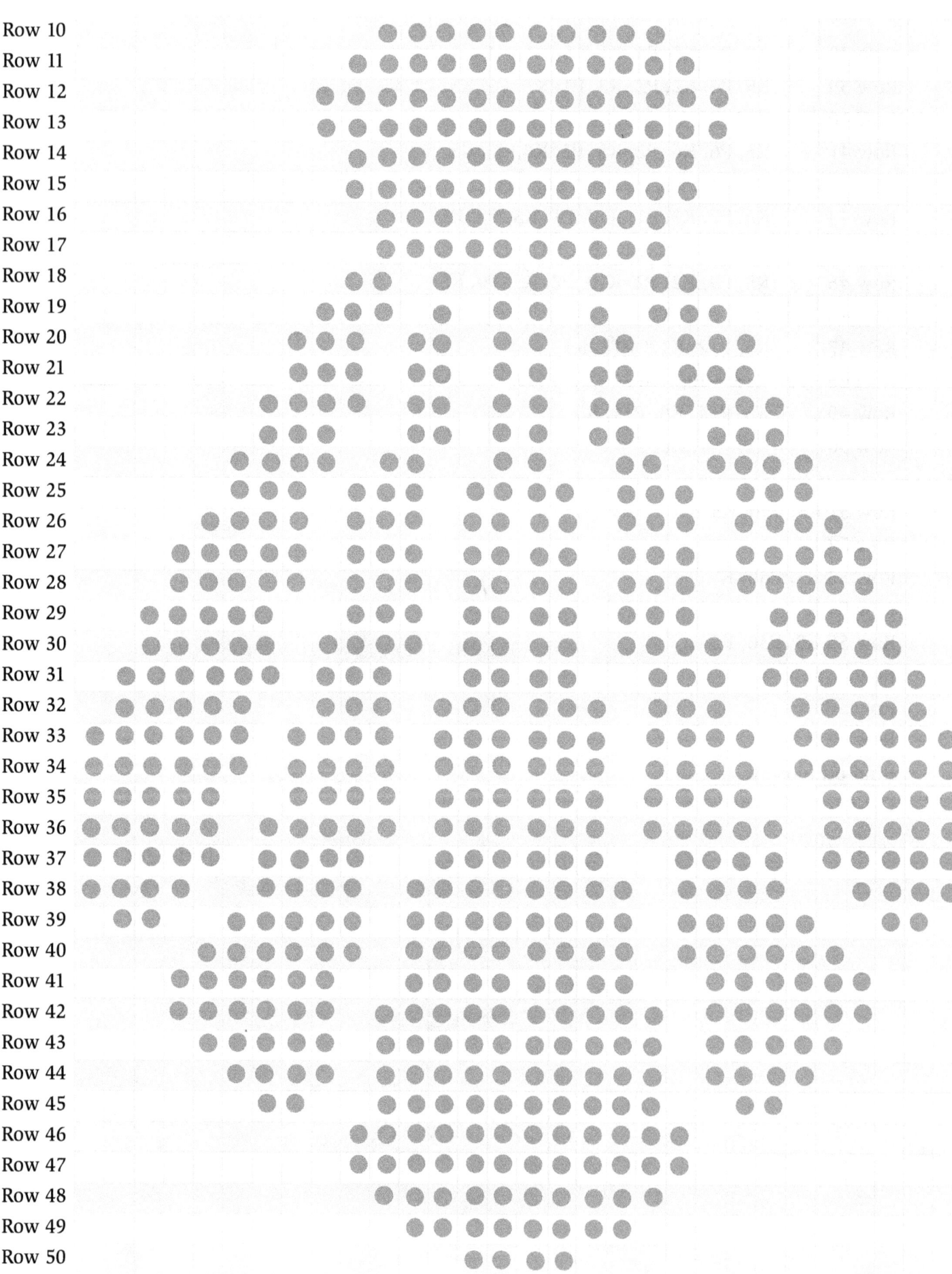

What Your Hand Finds to Do

Without God's provision, we would all starve and die. I know that's not a very cheery thought. Here's a more positive take on it: With God's gifts, we are fed, clothed, and cared for. He is the one who sends the rain and the sun to grow the grain in the fields. He is the one who gives good health to the farmer who tends and harvests that grain. He is the one who gives strength to the baker to pull that bread out of the oven. He provides the money for you to pay for the gasoline that gets you to the store to buy that loaf of bread. It's all from Him.

Unlike the ancient Israelites' manna, which rained down directly from heaven, our daily bread comes from God through earthly means. The farmer and the baker and the truck driver and the pizza delivery guy all work under God's direction so He can provide what we need. He uses our hands to handle the bag of apples, carry them home, chop them into small pieces and throw them into a salad or apple crumble for our families. He uses each person through various individual vocations to carry out His will of providing for the earth.

But because we do not receive our daily bread directly from heaven, we sometimes forget. We forget just how dependent on God we are for everything (Psalm 107:8–9). But if God withdrew His gifts to us, we'd quickly starve and die. And it's not only *food* that God gives. He orders the seasons; He sets the moon and the sun on their respective paths; and He creates our bodies with wisdom and order to keep us functioning in good health and wellness.

Vocation is, very simply, God working through people in the world to provide for one another. I often think of Richard Scarry's *Busytown*: all of the people doing their jobs, working in concert, in order to bring about good order in the community. The cement layer, carrying out his vocation, smooths out the concrete so people can get to work without falling on the sidewalk. The plumber, carrying out his vocation, watches the water swirl down the bathtub drain after unplugging it so that others can bathe and take care of their bodies. The pastor, carrying out his vocation, uses his voice to share God's Word and forgive the sinner. The teacher, carrying out her vocation, grades the papers that help the children see their mistakes and learn from them. Each person carries out the duties of vocation in order to serve other people.

Most people have several vocations. For example, I am a wife, a daughter, a mother, a sister, an aunt, a writer, a volunteer, a friend, a neighbor, a tutor, and a teacher. What are your vocations? When considering this, it's helpful to identify the top three or four vocations to concentrate on and then give some thought as to how you will divide your time and energy between those. We women tend to juggle a lot of vocations in our lives. On a seemingly daily basis, I have to decide which comes first: my vocation as church volunteer or my vocation as writer? or teacher? or mom? It's difficult to balance everything, especially when juggling several vocations at once.

This past week, in just one very small example, I had to decide if I was going to drive my son to baseball practice or help out with a supper before Bible study at church. I couldn't be two places at once, as much as I would have liked to be. So which would I choose? In part, the decision came down to logistics. Could my son get a ride with a friend? Yes. So I arranged the carpool and all was well. But the decision also came down to vocation. Was it more important that I get my son to practice or help with a church function? These sorts of decisions as to what comes first often come down to our priorities with our vocations.

In order to identify your vocations, look at your family first. Are your parents still alive? Then you are a daughter. Do you have children? Then you are a mother. Do you work outside your home? If so, then you should count those jobs as vocations. Are you on the altar guild at church? Then being a church volunteer is one of your vocations.

In your vocation, you do "whatever your hand finds to do" (Ecclesiastes 9:10) and serve those God puts in front of you to the best of your ability. Here are some examples of vocation:

- The mother changing her baby's diaper.
- The student writing a rough draft of an essay due the following week.
- The mail carrier sorting and delivering the mail.
- The son helping to wash and fold the laundry.
- The older sister holding her younger brother's hand as they cross the street.
- The pharmacist counting out the pills for a prescription.
- The pastor pouring water over the infant's head in Baptism.
- The sanitation worker emptying garbage.

- The cleaning professional making crisp, tight corners with the bedsheets.

Before the Reformation, in the Middle Ages, a vocation referred only to those who would go into "God's service" as priests, nuns, or monks. This was having a vocation; doing anything else was certainly not preferable. But Martin Luther helped shift attitudes about the meaning of this word and how we approach our life's work. As God's holy children, our work is sanctified through Christ and blessed merely because we are serving our neighbor.

All of these little tasks become elevated to godly behavior when we perceive them as working within our vocations. How do we serve our neighbors? By doing those tasks God has placed in our hands to do.

1. Read **Ecclesiastes 9:10**. What is the exhortation in the beginning of this verse?

2. List at least five things that "your hand finds to do" in a typical day.

3. Read **Ephesians 4:1–2**. Looking particularly at verse 2, how does St. Paul describe what our behavior toward others should look like?

4. Notice in **Ephesians 4:1–2** that St. Paul links humility and service toward others closely to our vocations, or callings. In light of this, consider what "callings" you have received. This is not so lofty as it may sound. A calling is, in essence, a vocation, or whatever "your hand finds to do." List three of your vocations. Then expand on that by explaining the crosses, privileges, and joys of each one.

   a.

   b.

   c.

5. Read **Colossians 3:18–25**. How does St. Paul sum up the teaching of vocation in this passage?

6. Before we reach out in love to others, we first must be strengthened in our relationship with God. He is the Giver; we are the receivers. He gives His kindness, forgiveness, and love, which we receive with nothing but an open hand. Read **Ephesians 2:1–9**. How are we saved? What does not save us?

7. Continue by reading **Ephesians 2:10**. After learning about God's love for us and His saving grace, what does verse 10 emphasize?

Digging Deeper

8. Do your vocations ever change? Describe an example of a vocation that does change, as well as one that might not.

9. How can thinking about vocation in this different light help you as you perform the humdrum duties of your everyday life?

10. How do you make the decision about which vocation takes precedence when there is a conflict?

11. When you are feeling unsatisfied in your life, can the understanding of vocation help you to become more content? Why or why not?

Verse to remember:

For we are His workmanship, created in Christ Jesus for good works, which God prepared beforehand, that we should walk in them.

Ephesians 2:10

Project: Bath Mitt

This mitt is intended to be used when washing a baby. Knitted from cotton, it allows for a firmer hold on soft, slippery skin and doesn't easily slip like a standard baby washcloth.

Skill level: Medium

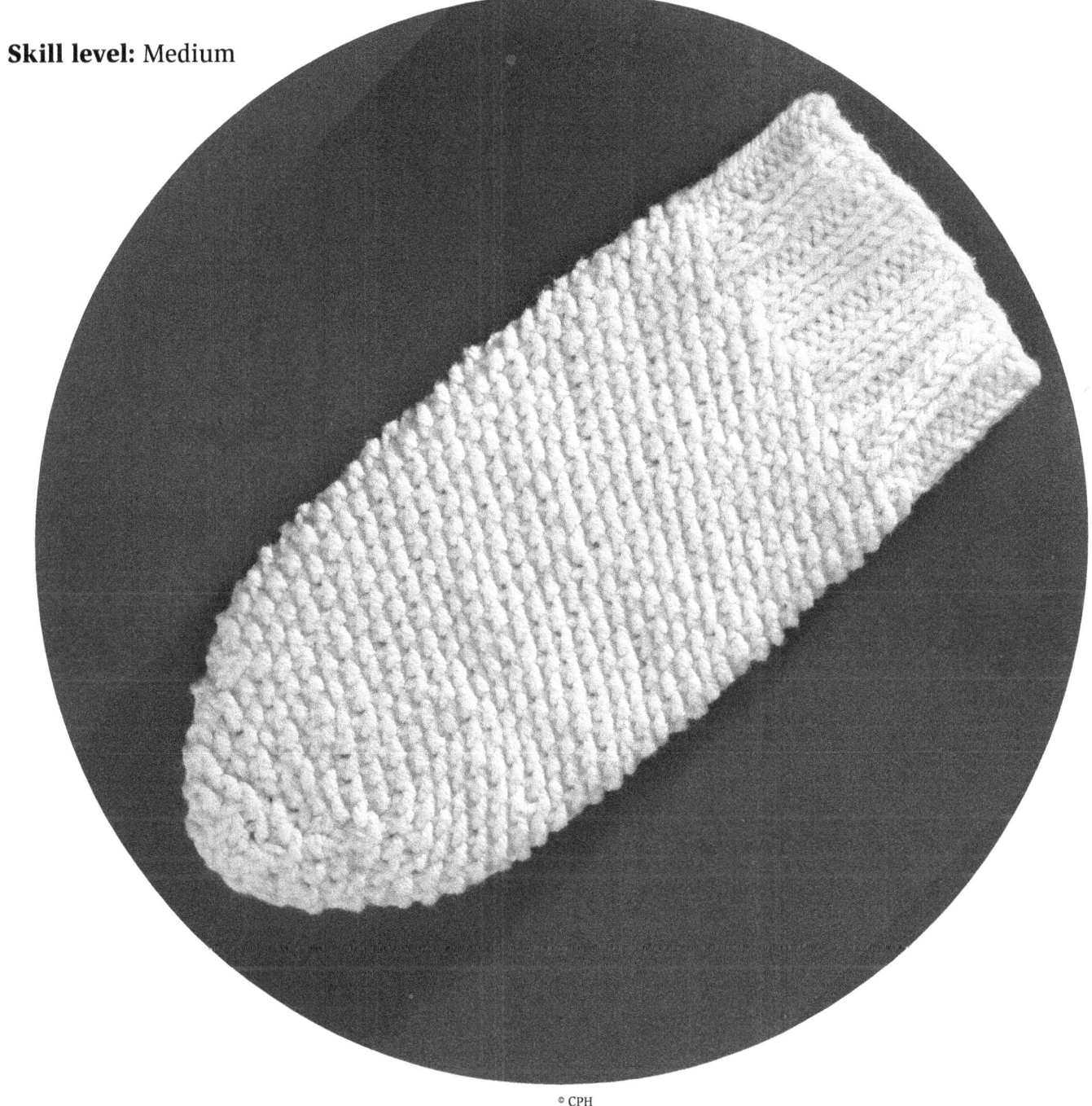

Needles: Set of 5 or 6 US size 5 DPNs; yarn needle for weaving in ends

Yarn: Cotton, such as Lily's Sugar and Cream, or weight that gives similar gauge

Gauge: 2" × 2" 9 stitches and 13 rows in pattern

Finished size: Adult size medium

Cast on 36 stitches, distribute across four needles and join in a round, being careful not to twist.

Cuff

*K2, P2. Repeat from * to end. Continue until cuff measures at least 2".

Body

Increase 1 (knit into back of first stitch but do not take off needle; purl in front of the same stitch; slip to needle) to make 37 stitches. Knit in pattern: K1 through the back loop, P1 until mitt is 6" beyond the cuff.

Begin decrease. Continue with stitch pattern but decrease one stitch in the round.

First decrease row: *K4 in established pattern, then K2tog. Continue from * to end of row.

Knit 2 rows in established pattern.

Next decrease row: *K3 in established pattern, then K2tog. Continue from * to end of row.

Knit 2 rows in established pattern.

Next decrease row: *K2 in established pattern, then K2tog. Continue from * to end of row.

Knit 2 rows in established pattern.

Next decrease row: *K1, K2tog. Continue from * to end of row.

Knit 1 row in established pattern.

Last row: K2tog to end.

Cut yarn and use a yarn needle to thread yarn end through remaining stitches on needles; fasten off.

Note: At times, it will be tricky to follow the pattern. Use as your guide that each stitch needs to be the opposite type of the one that is below it.

Option

Begin knitting in stockinette stitch with first decrease row. Continue knitting in the round, decreasing as directed above.

Numbering the Hairs on Our Heads

Session 8

This study began with an in-depth look at Psalm 139: "O Lord, You have searched me and known me!" God truly knows us, each and every part of us, from before we were born—"My frame was not hidden from You, when I was being made in secret, intricately woven in the depths of the earth" (v. 15)—until the end of our days—"and lead me in the way everlasting" (v. 24).

We've discussed God's care for His children (His sheep) and His sheltering presence. We've covered Baptism and the Lord's Supper. We've pondered our vocations and contentment within them.

The reassurance of this psalm helps us through the dark days when we feel alone and lost and on our own. It connects us to our Creator, our Maker, who formed us and knows us better than anyone.

My blonde hair has been my distinguishing feature since the day I was born. My dad tells me that when I was a newborn, my head was covered with silvery blonde hair. As a child, it was light blonde, and it never darkened. Of course, because it's mine, I don't normally think about the fact that it's a bit unusual.

It's just the way I am, so I never really think about it except when I get my hair cut. Every time I go to a salon, someone asks, "Is that your color natural?" When I answer yes, I always hear, "People spend a lot of money for hair that color!" So, I guess it's my God-given bargain in life.

This distinguishing feature, I thought, would always help my young son identify me if we ever became separated in a crowd. But when my son was about four years old, my father-in-law grilled him on what he would do if he got lost. How would he describe me? He replied that he would tell people I was the "nice lady." Out of the mouths of babes!

What are your distinguishing features? Think of God's knowledge of you and all of those small things that make you unique. Your laugh, your height, your quick wit, your easy ability to talk to strangers, your eye color, your hair. What is it that makes you unique? Your closest friends and family members know these things about you. They see your ability to organize big events, your calm nature, your devotion to your children, your resilience, or your generous heart toward those around you. But think about all of the things they don't know about you, about your interior life, your inner conversations, your fears, your hopes, your resentments. But God knows all of these things, doesn't He?

Let's look at a few more verses to describe the way God knows us from the tips of our toes to the tops of our heads.

1. Read **Matthew 10:30**. How does this verse describe how God knows us?

2. Now read the surrounding verses, **Matthew 10:28–33**. Jesus says that we need not fear. What is the reason He gives for this?

3. The project for this lesson is a hat, so it seemed appropriate to discuss God's creation from our feet to our "crowns." In **Isaiah 35:10**, what will cover our heads? As we "come to Zion with singing," what will happen?

4. More verses about "crowns" are scattered throughout the Bible. Most refer to how God treasures and cherishes His people. Read **Isaiah 62:2–5** and describe God's attitude toward His people in these verses.

5. Other verses describe being "crowned" with certain qualities or blessings. Name the blessings from these verses:
   a. **Psalm 103:4**

   b. **Psalm 8:4–5**

   c. **2 Timothy 4:8**

75

Digging Deeper

6. Luther described the substitution of Jesus' righteousness for our sinfulness as a "blessed exchange." This exchange can be represented by another set of crowns: we are *crowned* with blessing and honor, while Jesus wears a different *crown*. Read **John 19:5** and describe the scene.

7. Then read **Philippians 2:4–11** and describe the final scene outlined in this passage.

8. This lesson focuses on how God knows us from the tips of our toes to the tops of our crowns. He numbers the hairs on our heads. God's perfect knowledge of us, His children, can reassure us that He is caring for us like the loving, protective Father He is. How can this reassurance help you in the coming week? the coming day? right now?

9. Are there times in your life when you find it easier to trust in God's unfailing love? times when it's more difficult? Why do you think this is so?

10. Read **Revelation 2:10**. What is the crown that the faithful receive? How is this meaningful or significant to you? What blessed reassurance God gives us in this verse!

Verse to remember:

Be faithful unto death, and I will give you the crown of life.
Revelation 2:10

Project: Difficult Hat

Skill level: Intermediate/Advanced

Needles: Set of 5 or 6 US size 5 DPNs; yarn needle for weaving in ends

Yarn: Bernat Softee Baby or weight that gives similar gauge

Gauge: 2" × 2" 12 stitches and 14 rows in pattern

Finished size: Preemie (8" circumference at bottom, not stretched)

Cast on 60 stitches. Divide evenly across four or five needles. Place marker and join in the round, being careful not to twist.

Pattern

Row 1: *P2, K second stitch, do not slip off needle, K first stitch, slip both to right needle, K1. Repeat from * to end of row.

Row 2: *P2, K1, K second stitch, do not slip off needle, K first stitch, slip both to right needle. Repeat from * to end of row.

Continue in pattern until hat measures 5"; end with row 2.

Decrease

Row 1: *P2tog, K second stitch, do not slip off needle, K first stitch, slip both to right needle, K1. Repeat from * to end of row.

Row 2: *P2tog, K second stitch, do not slip off needle, K first stitch, slip both to right needle. Repeat from * to end of row.

Row 3: *P1, K2 tog. Continue from * to end.

Rows 4 and 5: *K2 tog. Continue from * to end.

Finish: Break yarn and use a yarn needle to slip through remaining 6 stitches. Fasten off. Weave in ends.

Note: For a larger size hat (10½" circumference), cast on 80 stitches.

Practice your eight "verses to remember" from the end of each lesson. Consider writing the verses on small cards and making pouches to hold the verse cards so you can carry them with you as you continue to memorize them. Karen, from my Bible study group, made felt pouches with pockets on each side for every one of us in the group. This could be an easy project for your group to make either for yourselves or for your congregation. Having this pouch on my nightstand encourages me to look at it morning and evening to review the verses.

To make your pouches, cut a piece of felt approximately 8" × 4". Fold the two ends toward the middle to create two pockets for your cards. The pockets should be approximately 1½" × 4". Sew along the long sides of felt to secure your pockets. Voila! Instant Bible-memory-verse pouch! Cut index cards into smaller sizes (approximately 1½" × 3") that will fit into the pockets. You can put verses you are learning on one side of the pouch and verses you've already memorized on the other.

By faith we understand that the universe was created
by the word of God, so that what is seen was not made
out of things that are visible. **Hebrews 11:3**

For as many of you as were baptized into Christ
have put on Christ. **Galatians 3:27**

Baptism . . . now saves you,
not as a removal of dirt from the body
but as an appeal to God for a good conscience. **1 Peter 3:21**

The thief comes only to steal and kill and destroy.
I came that they may have life and have it abundantly. **John 10:10**

He who dwells in the shelter of the Most High
    will abide in the shadow of the Almighty.
I will say to the LORD,
"My refuge and my fortress, my God, in whom I trust." Psalm 91:1-2

Looking to Jesus, the founder and perfecter of our faith,
    who for the joy that was set before Him endured the cross,
despising the shame, and is seated at the right hand
        of the throne of God. Hebrews 12:2

For we are His workmanship, created in Christ Jesus
    for good works, which God prepared beforehand,
        that we should walk in them. Ephesians 2:10

Be faithful unto death, and I will give you
        the crown of life. Revelation 2:10.

leader's notes

Session 1

1. The earth was formless and empty; darkness was over the surface of the deep.
2. Light [Day]; darkness [Night]; sky [Heaven]; Earth; Seas; vegetation; sun; moon; all sea creatures; birds; livestock; creeping things; beasts of the earth; man.
3. Creation is described as very good.
4. God created the world and living creatures with His words, His voice. God formed the man of dust from the ground and breathed into his nostrils the breath of life. Eve was taken from one of Adam's ribs.
5. We were created in God's own image.
6. Answers will vary.
7. Answers will vary.
8. It is by faith we believe that God created the world. Without faith, people do not believe in God's creative work.
9. Our Father.
10. The mind is hostile to God and does not and cannot submit to God's Law.
11. We can call ourselves children of God because in Christ Jesus we are sons of God through faith and Baptism.
12. Jesus reconciled us to God through His death. As both God and man, Christ Jesus paid for our sins. He is our means of forgiveness, fully and finally satisfying our need for atonement.
13. God is our Father, our potter, our Maker.
14. Answers will vary.
15. Answers will vary.

Session 2

1. Answers will vary. Each of us is uniquely created.
2. God has known us since conception, and even before that. It can be comforting to know that God is our Maker, who has known us from all eternity.
3. Answers will vary.
4. We enter the world with nothing; we leave with nothing.
5. The robe signified the favor that Jacob, their father, showed to Joseph.
6. The brothers strip Joseph of his robe, throw him into a well, and then sell him to Ishmaelites, who in turn sell him into slavery to Egypt.
7. The theme is that of forgiveness, that God can bring good from evil, and that God is always in charge.
8. Jesus gave Himself for us to purify us from all sin.
9. Through Baptism, we are clothed with Christ. We are robed in garments of salvation and in robes of righteousness.
10. Answers will vary. Our perspective sometimes is skewed by our own feelings or emotions; however, God's ways are not our own. We need to view the world—and ourselves—through the lenses of God's grace and mercy.
11. Answers will vary.
12. Answers will vary. God does not condemn us; even more, He graciously wraps a robe of righteousness around us. He does not see the sins we have committed. We can rest in the assurance of God's grace.
13. Answers will vary. Sometimes when there is grievous wrong done to us, we can find it extremely difficult to forgive. It's also more difficult, humanly speaking, when we have been wronged repeatedly by the same person. Especially in these sorts of situations, we need to rely on God's strength. He does not hold our sins against us. Neither should we hold wrongs committed against us.
14. Answers will vary.

Session 3

1. Baptism is receiving the Father (having God as one's gracious Father) and the Son (receiving all of the benefits of the Son's redeeming acts) and the Holy Spirit (receiving the life-giving, life-sustaining power and presence of the Holy Spirit). Baptism is the enacted Gospel of the Trinity.

2. Baptism is the doorway through which we receive salvation.

3. Baptism washes away our sin and gives us a membership into God's family. We become His adopted children.

4. Noah's Ark/Flood: Floodwaters were used to destroy; God sent His judgment on the earth; the ark saved those who believed. Baptism: Used to save us from eternal death; applies the benefits of Jesus' death for our sins; saves us from sins. Noah and his family started a new life after leaving the ark. We are given new life in Baptism and are welcomed into God's family. Also, in Genesis 9:8–17, God establishes a new covenant, entrusts the care of the earth and its creatures to Noah and his family, and gives a sign (rainbow). Baptism is a covenant of sorts between the parents/godparents/congregation and God to support this new believer in his or her walk and help the person "grow" in faith. We are also given the sign of the cross and water in Baptism.

5. The Ethiopian was reading the Old Testament Book of Isaiah, the prophet.

6. The Ethiopian said, "How can I [understand it], unless someone guides me?"

7. The kingdom belongs to all who have a trusting, childlike faith and who receive the kingdom of God as a gift freely given. It is for any believer, near or far.

8. The three drops of water symbolize the Father, Son, and Holy Spirit. The image of the three drops of water relates to the life-giving gifts of the Holy Trinity, which are applied to us in Baptism. We are adopted into God the Father's family because the Son died on the cross so we could be saved. Finally, we are given the gift of the life-sustaining presence of the Holy Spirit, who helps to guide and nurture us as we grow in faith.

9. This might be a fun discussion for your group. Most families choose to have sponsors or godparents involved who promise to help encourage the newly baptized to continue growing in faith. Other traditions are to have a large family party afterward. Often for infant Baptisms, there may be a special baptismal gown handed down from other family members. These traditions can help you "relive" the blessings that your Baptism continues to bring you as a believer. Luther connected the waters of Baptism to our daily use of water in washing to help us remember and appreciate the blessings of Baptism.

Session 4

1. There is total trust between the sheep and the shepherd. The shepherd cares for the sheep and the sheep do not hesitate to follow him.
2. The shepherd goes out in front of the sheep to lead them. This is different from Western shepherds, who guide their sheep by corralling them from behind.
3. The Lord is compassionate and gentle. He leads us tenderly by calling us by name and speaking to us through His Word.
4. The sheep follow the voice of their shepherd. They recognize his voice.
5. In times of illness, disappointment, frustration, or crisis, we find it natural to cry out to God, to know our limits as we seek God's assistance.
6. A hired hand does not care for the sheep the way that the shepherd does. The shepherd cares for the sheep with compassion, never letting even one little lamb stray.
7. A good shepherd knows his sheep and his sheep know him. The shepherd lays down his life for the sheep.
8. Jesus laid down His life of His own accord. No one took His life from Him, but He laid it down for us.
9. Answers will vary.

Session 5

1.a. A shelter is somewhere to hide from the storm, such as some sort of building or strong structure that provides protection.

1.b. God is our shelter by His powerful presence, providing protection from life's storms.

2.a. The word *shadow* brings to mind sitting under a shade tree on a hot summer day and the relief the tree gives you from the sun beating down.

2.b. God is like a shadow that provides needed rest, shelter, and refreshment to us.

3.a. The word *refuge* makes us think of a refugee fleeing a war-torn country, finally escaping and finding refuge in a safe shelter.

3.b. God gives us refuge—haven or protection for us when problems of this world and our own sin threaten us.

4.a. The word *fortress* brings up military imagery of a rocky or thick-walled safe haven that keeps enemies at bay.

4.b. God, our Fortress, protects us from the assaults of the devil, the world, and our flesh.

5. The beautiful imagery of these verses describes the Lord's protective covering over His children. Under His wings of protection, we are safely gathered together, protected from the devil's slings and arrows.

6. These verses bring great comfort. We know that we are kept safe from the wiles of the evil one as we are in the protection of our God.

7. Psalms 31:14 and 37:5 describe the believer's attitude of trust in God.

8. *Faith* is another word for trust. The tender trust/faith of the believer is her foremost thought and heart attitude as she leans on the Lord for His care, protection, and guidance.

9. The Holy Spirit Himself grants us faith to trust in God. Without Him and His calling, enlightenment, and safe-keeping, we would be lost in our sin and hostile toward the Gospel. But the Holy Spirit creates faith within us and nurtures us in the faith.

10. The angels do the Lord's bidding; the angels also guard us and lift us up.

11. These last verses summarize God's care. We call upon God, and He answers us. He delivers us, He is with us in trouble, and He will satisfy us with salvation.

12. Some actions we could take to remember God's love and care are to review Bible verses that reassure us of His care, to attend worship regularly, and to engage in fellowship activities that will remind us of God's compassion.

13. Answers will vary.

14. Answers will vary.

Session 6

1. Baptism is effective because it is given by God—"He saved us . . . by the washing of regeneration and renewal of the Holy Spirit." God makes us holy through the washing He Himself effects.
2. Baptism makes us holy, gives us hope, and grants us eternal life.
3. Jesus' blood was poured out for the forgiveness of sins.
4. The blood of Jesus purifies us from all sin. The Lord's Supper makes us die to sin and live for righteousness.
5. "Without the shedding of blood, there is no forgiveness of sins."
6. Forgiveness comes to us only through God's grace.
7. God gives us faith, into our lowly "jars of clay." We house the faith that God gives.
8. This treasure is the promise of salvation.
9. Like jars of clay, we are fragile, breakable. Our bodies are earthly vessels.
10. Because Christ dwells in us, we are living temples of God.
11. Answers will vary.
12. Answers will vary, but could include sharing the good news of salvation with others, caring for children, and loving family members.

Session 7

1. The exhortation at the beginning of Ecclesiastes 9:10 is to identify "whatever your hand finds to do."
2. Answers will vary, but could include things such as sorting the mail, typing an e-mail, washing dishes, changing a diaper, holding a child's hand, and giving a back rub to a tension-filled spouse.
3. According to Ephesians 4:1–2, we should be gentle, humble, and patient, bearing with others in love.
4. Answers will vary, but might resemble the following: Mother: care for son when he is sick; make sure he is doing his homework; provide opportunities for daily Bible reading; bring child to church weekly. Teacher: show compassion and understanding to my students; prepare lessons that help students grow in knowledge; work with colleagues in a manner worthy of the Gospel.
5. Paul gives specific guidelines for family roles, and then in verse 23 goes on to say that whatever we do, we should work as though we were working for the Lord and not for men.
6. Because of God's great love for us in Christ, we are saved by grace, not by our own good works or merit. This comes by grace through faith. It is not of ourselves so that no one can boast.
7. Ephesians 2:10 emphasizes the fact that we are created in Christ; we are His workmanship. We are created to do good works and they are prepared for us in advance to do.
8. Yes, vocations can and do change. Even though I will never cease being a mother, my work for my children changes as they get older, more independent, and then finally move away from home. I will always be a daughter, but if my parents are no longer living, then my actions and life will also change. Retiring, moving, or resigning from jobs could cause a change in vocations.
9. Answers will vary, but should include that we give honor and glory to God in all we do, regardless how humble or lowly our work.
10. Answers will vary.
11. Answers will vary. Because we are made righteous by Christ, our work is to His glory. We may not see the results of our work in our lifetime, but we can be confident that the Lord will bless that work and multiply it in His time and according to His purpose.

Session 8

1. Matthew 10:30 shows that God knows us so perfectly that He even numbers the hairs on our head. This demonstrates that God knows us better than any person ever could, or even better than we know ourselves.
2. The surrounding verses describe the fact that we need not fear anyone or anything that could harm our bodies. Instead, we have a healthy fear of God, realizing that to Him we owe our perfect obedience and faith.
3. Isaiah 35:10 says that as we come to Zion, where everlasting joy shall be upon our heads, we shall obtain gladness and joy, and sorrow and sighing shall flee away.
4. From Isaiah 62, we learn that God delights in us. We are treasured and cherished by God's gracious love.
5.a. Psalm 103:4: We are crowned with steadfast love and mercy.
5.b. Psalm 8:4–5: We are crowned with glory and honor, and given a position in the Kingdom that is just a little lower than that of the angels.
5.c. 2 Timothy 4:8: We will be given the crown of righteousness.
6. In John 19, we see Jesus wearing the crown of thorns and the purple robe. Jesus was humbled and brought low in order to pay for the penalty of our sins.
7. On the Last Day, Jesus will be exalted and glorified (Philippians 2). Before Him, every knee on heaven and earth will bow.
8. Answers will vary.
9. Answers will vary.
10. Answers will vary.

www.ingramcontent.com/pod-product-compliance
Lightning Source LLC
Chambersburg PA
CBHW080924170426
43201CB00016B/2261